Motorcycles

Lisa Jane Gillespie

Designed by Anna Gould

Illustrated by Emmanuel Cerisier, John Fox, Adrian Dean and Adrian Roots

Edited by Alex Frith and Jane Chisholm

Motorcycles experts: Damien Kimberley, Coventry Transport Museum
and Neil Symington, Riverside Museum – Scotland's Museum of Travel and Transport

Contents

Bikers kick up mud as they scramble around the first corner of the British Motocross Championships, 2009.

Which motorcycle?

Motorcycles are fast, powerful and easy to maneuver. Some are built for speed; others for style – but they all have the same basic parts.

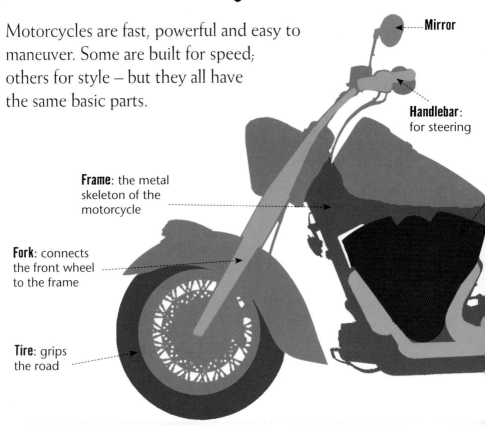

Mirror

Handlebar: for steering

Frame: the metal skeleton of the motorcycle

Fork: connects the front wheel to the frame

Tire: grips the road

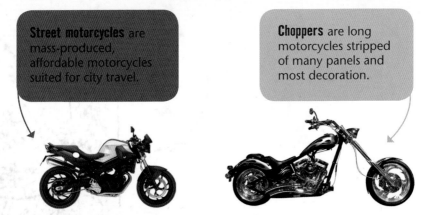

Street motorcycles are mass-produced, affordable motorcycles suited for city travel.

Choppers are long motorcycles stripped of many panels and most decoration.

Engine: powers the motorcycle

Seat: where the biker sits

Exhaust: carries away waste gas

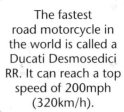

The fastest road motorcycle in the world is called a Ducati Desmosedici RR. It can reach a top speed of 200mph (320km/h).

Cruisers are stylish street motorcycles that are often colorful and personalized, based on old, classic motorcycle styles.

Sports bikes are built for speed. They're made of light materials and have powerful engines.

Touring motorcycles have strong engines and large fuel tanks for long distance rides.

Dirt bikes are used for racing on off-road tracks of grass, sand, ice and mud.

Racing motorcycles

Motorcycle riders race in all sorts of places – from huge stadiums to rocky mountains. Each course has different challenges.

These professionals are competing in a motorcycle Grand Prix race on the racetrack at the Mazda Raceway Laguna Seca in California.

Motorcycle Grand Prix racing is also known as MotoGP. The motorcycles typically reach speeds of about 185mph (300km/h).

Motorcycles for courses

Different kinds of motorcycles are used in different types of racing depending on whether the surface is sand, asphalt, grass, mud or even ice.

Type of race	Famous races	Type of bike
Road racing – on road courses, often over hills and around difficult sequences of corners	Isle of Man TT, see pages 36-37	Sport bikes
Track racing – around stadium courses, on various surfaces, with a mixture of straights and turns	MotoGP; Speedway, see pages 46-47	Sport bikes, dirt bikes, and ultra fast sport bikes known as super motorcycles
Endurance, Rally raids – on off-road routes, over mud and grass, often for hours at a time	Dawn til' Dusk races; Dakar rally see pages 52-55	Modified sport and dirt bikes
Motocross, Scrambling – on muddy or rocky courses	FIM Grand Prix, see pages 48-49	Dirt bikes
Ice racing – around snow and ice tracks	Iceway, see pages 50-51	Modified dirt bikes
Land speed – races to set records for super fast travel	Bonneville Salt Flats, Utah, USA, see pages 66-67	Aerodynamic motorcycles, designed to be extremely fast
Hill climbing – around obstacle routes involving rocks and streams	Pikes Peak, Colorado, USA	Modified dirt bikes

Building bikes

Most motorcycles are built in large factories, on high-tech production lines. A few are built by hand in workshops by small teams of experts.

These motorcycles are being assembled in the Harley-Davidson Vehicle Operations department in Pennsylvania, USA.

Tricky terrains

Unlike most cars, motorcycles are so powerful and easy to maneuver that they can travel over different types of surfaces, or terrains, from rocky hillsides to riverbanks.

The first motorcycles were nicknamed 'mechanical horses'.

Water
This biker is powering through a river. The engine is high up so the water doesn't get in and damage it.

Ice
Special spiked tires stop the motorcycle from sliding and falling over on icy surfaces.

Mountains
Bikers can steer around rocks on mountain terrain, and the motorcycle's tires grip the stones.

Mud
A car might sink into mud, but a motorcycle is light and fast enough to travel through it.

Sand
Bikers can use special 'paddle' tires for riding on sand. They're knobbed and don't get clogged up easily.

Riding gear

Bikers wear tough clothing and strong safety gear to protect themselves from injury in falls and crashes.

Most **jackets** are made from Kevlar, a man-made material that won't scrape or tear if the rider falls onto a rough surface while riding at high speeds.

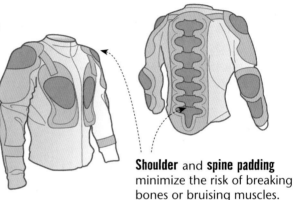

Shoulder and **spine padding** minimize the risk of breaking bones or bruising muscles.

Tough **gloves** protect the rider's hands from injury and the weather, but don't interfere with operating the controls.

Pants made from Kevlar protect the rider's legs.

Riders wear **layers** under their outer gear – thermals to keep warm in the cold, or light layers of breathable fabrics to keep cool in the heat.

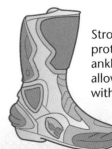

Strong, heavy **boots** protect the rider's ankles and feet but allow firm contact with the pedals.

Helmets

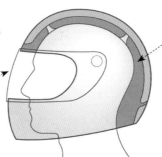

A biker's helmet is made of light, strong fiberglass and carbon fiber.

The visor protects the rider's face from bugs, dust and stones.

A casing inside the helmet protects the rider's head from knocks and bumps, preventing brain damage in case of a fall.

Knee and **elbow braces** – molded pieces of plastic that slot around the joint – reduce the risk of breaking bones in a fall.

The engine

Inside motorcycle engines are cylinders containing fuel that is used to drive pistons up and down. This piston motion is what powers the motorcycle.

How the engine works

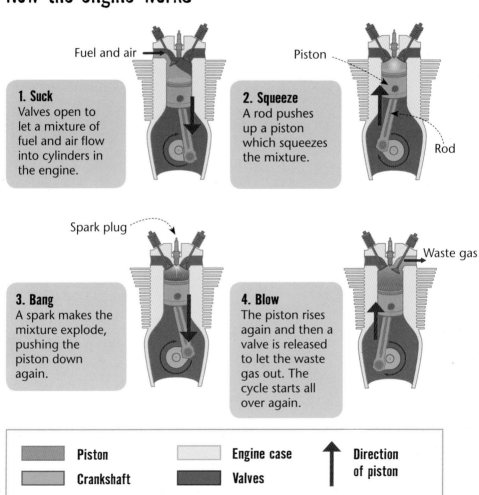

Fuel and air

Piston

1. Suck
Valves open to let a mixture of fuel and air flow into cylinders in the engine.

2. Squeeze
A rod pushes up a piston which squeezes the mixture.

Rod

Spark plug

Waste gas

3. Bang
A spark makes the mixture explode, pushing the piston down again.

4. Blow
The piston rises again and then a valve is released to let the waste gas out. The cycle starts all over again.

Piston	Engine case	**Direction of piston**
Crankshaft	Valves	

Turning the wheels

The movement of the pistons turns a piece of metal called the crankshaft. The crankshaft carries power to the gearbox that turns the drive system. This powers the rear wheel.

	Engine case
	Cylinder
	Piston
	Crankshaft
	Gearbox
	Drive system

This engine is known as a V2 or a V twin, because it has two cylinders arranged in a V shape.

The front wheel spins freely, pushed forward by the engine driving the rear wheel.

As the pistons move up and down, they turn the crankshaft.

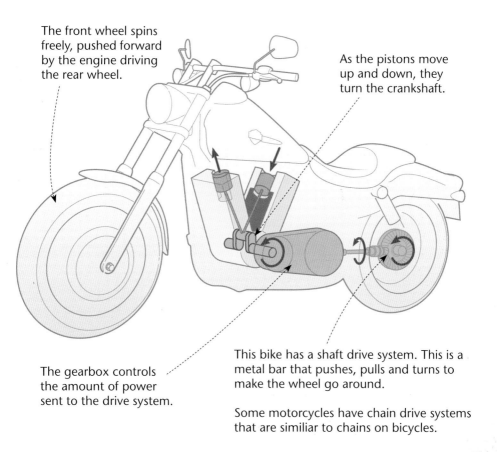

The gearbox controls the amount of power sent to the drive system.

This bike has a shaft drive system. This is a metal bar that pushes, pulls and turns to make the wheel go around.

Some motorcycles have chain drive systems that are similiar to chains on bicycles.

Engine layout

Engines can have anything from one to eight cylinders, arranged singly, in rows, or in V shapes. You can often tell how many cylinders an engine has because they're shiny and on show.

Here are four examples of the many possible engine arrangements:

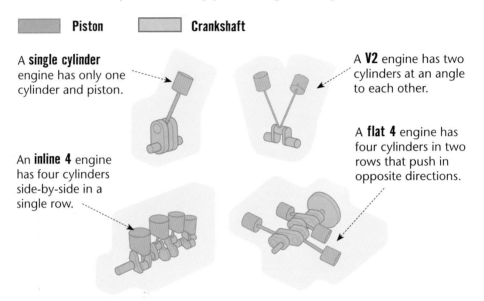

■ **Piston**   □ **Crankshaft**

A **single cylinder** engine has only one cylinder and piston.

A **V2** engine has two cylinders at an angle to each other.

A **flat 4** engine has four cylinders in two rows that push in opposite directions.

An **inline 4** engine has four cylinders side-by-side in a single row.

Motorcycle power

A bike's power is defined in *bhp* at *rpm*. *Bhp* stands for 'brake horsepower' and *rpm* for 'revolutions per minute' – the number of times a minute the crankshaft turns.

Horsepower compares the power of engines to the power of horses. It was invented when engines replaced horses for work and travel, so people could understand how powerful the engine was.

A dial on the motorcycle's controls gives that moment's rpm reading. This dial shows 11,000rpm.

Comparing engines					
Motorcycle	Weight	Cylinders	Capacity	Max. power	Top speed
Scooter	331lbs (150kg)	1	125cc	15bhp at 9,750rpm	62mph (100km/h)
Super motorcycle	408lbs (185kg)	V2	1,150cc	150bhp at 10,000rpm	171mph (275km/h)
Cruiser	728lbs (330kg)	V2	1,720cc	74bhp at 4,500rpm	124mph (200km/h)
Sport bike	331lbs (150kg)	inline 4	790cc	200bhp at 23,000rpm	186mph (300km/h)
Touring bike	794lbs (360kg)	flat 6	1,850cc	120bhp at 5,500rpm	121mph (195km/h)
Dirt bike	212lbs (96kg)	1	250cc	40bhp at 13,500rpm	75mph (121km/h)

The number of cylinders and their arrangement differs from company to company. For example, Harley-Davidson only uses V2 engines.

The total amount of fuel and air drawn into the cylinders during one engine cycle is known as the capacity. It's measured in cubic centimeters (cc).

In the seat

Riding a motorcycle takes concentration, care and coordination. A rider must balance, operate the controls and steer – all at the same time.

The rider of this powerful sport motorcycle, a Suzuki GSX-R750, is leaning over to balance the motorcycle, so it doesn't topple over as it turns the corner. He is leaning so far that his knee is almost touching the ground.

Motorcycle controls

All motorcycles have the same controls, although they're not always in the same places. Here is a typical set of controls.

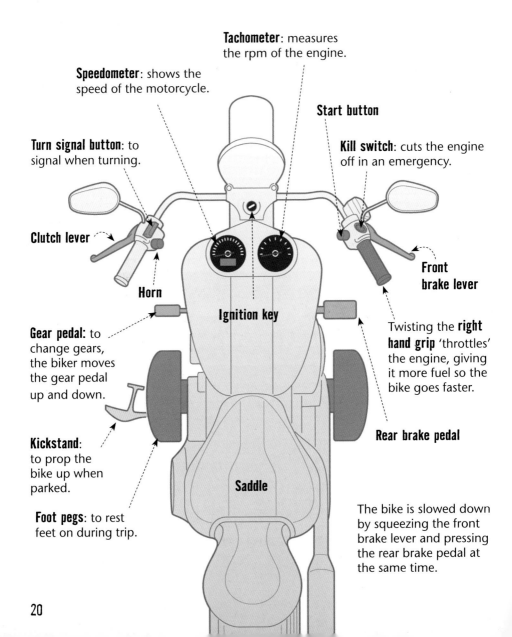

Tachometer: measures the rpm of the engine.

Speedometer: shows the speed of the motorcycle.

Start button

Turn signal button: to signal when turning.

Kill switch: cuts the engine off in an emergency.

Clutch lever

Front brake lever

Horn

Ignition key

Gear pedal: to change gears, the biker moves the gear pedal up and down.

Twisting the **right hand grip** 'throttles' the engine, giving it more fuel so the bike goes faster.

Rear brake pedal

Kickstand: to prop the bike up when parked.

Saddle

Foot pegs: to rest feet on during trip.

The bike is slowed down by squeezing the front brake lever and pressing the rear brake pedal at the same time.

Turning corners

Motorcycles need to be handled differently at different speeds. To turn a corner at low speeds, the rider turns the handlebars in the direction of the bend.

The biker leans over slightly with the bike to help balance it...

...and steers into the direction of the turn.

The rider turns the handlebars in the opposite direction to the bend...

...and leans strongly into the turn.

At high speeds, the rider turns the handlebars in the opposite direction of the bend. This is called counter steering. It's necessary because motorcycle tires spin very quickly and wobble a little when the bike is moving fast.

Bumps and brakes

A motorcycle relies on different systems working together to run smoothly. The two most important systems are the suspension and brakes.

Suspension   **Brakes**

How suspension works

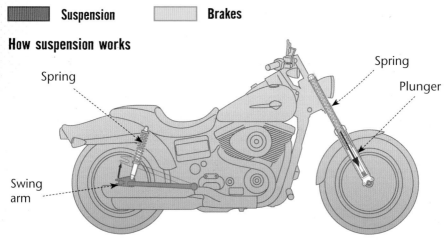

Spring

Spring

Plunger

Swing arm

A swing arm is attached to the frame. A spring allows it to swing up and down gently to absorb shocks.

To absorb a shock, a plunger moves into a column of oil, then a spring returns it slowly to its original place.

How brakes work

Disc brakes

Drum brakes

Drum brakes expand and press against the rear wheel. This gently stops it from turning.

Disc brakes pinch part of the front wheel. This quickly stops it from turning.

This new BMW motorcycle has reached the end of the production line. It will now be tested to make sure it's stable and safe to ride.

Street motorcycles

Street motorcycles, sometimes called standard motorcycles, are the ones you'll see most often. With medium-sized engines, they're suited to city life and are often used for making deliveries.

TDM900
(Yamaha Motor Company, Japan, 2010)

- **Engine:** 897cc, inline 2 cylinder
- **Weight:** 492lbs (223kg)
- **Power:** 86bhp at 7,500rpm

This is the usual riding position for a street biker.

Lights, mirror and a horn help the rider move through traffic.

A muffler fitted to the exhaust reduces its noise.

The tread patterns on the tires allow them to grip dry and wet road surfaces well.

The frame is made from aluminum, which is strong and light.

F 800 R
(BMW Motorrad, Germany, 2011)

- **Engine:** 798cc, inline 2 cylinder
- **Weight:** 375lbs (170kg)
- **Power:** 86bhp at 8,000rpm

Splendor
(Hero Honda, India, since 1994)

- **Engine:** 97cc, single cylinder
- **Weight:** 240lbs (109kg)
- **Power:** 75bhp at 8,000rpm

Over 8 million Splendor motorcycles have been sold, making them the biggest-selling motorcycles ever.

Scooters have small engines. They're easier to learn to ride than bigger motorcycles.

Vespa GTS 125 Super
(Piaggio, Italy, 2009)

- **Engine:** 124cc, single cylinder
- **Weight:** 333lbs (151kg)
- **Power:** 15bhp at 9,750rpm

Touring motorcycles

Touring motorcycles were developed for long distance road trips across the USA. These heavy motorcycles have large fuel tanks, powerful engines, extra storage space and wide windshields.

VN1700 Voyager (Kawasaki, Japan, 2009)
- **Engine:** 1,700cc, V2
- **Weight:** 895lbs (406kg)
- **Power:** 74bhp at 5,000rpm

Touring motorcycles can easily carry passengers.

Antenna for radio

Room for two people to travel in comfort

Wide windshield

Huge headlights

Lots of space for luggage

GL1800 Goldwing
(Honda, Japan, 2001)

- **Engine:** 1,832cc, flat 6 cylinder
- **Weight:** 800lbs (363kg)
- **Power:** 117bhp at 5,500rpm

Honda Goldwings are often used as official vehicles for traffic police in the USA.

Sprint GT (Triumph, UK, 2011)

- **Engine:** 1,050cc, inline 3 cylinder
- **Weight:** 589lbs (268kg)
- **Power:** 128bhp at 9,200rpm

The GT in the Sprint's name stands for 'Grand Tourer'. These motorcycles can carry enough fuel for a 200 mile (320km) journey.

Electra Glide Ultra Limited
(Harley–Davidson, USA, 2011)

- **Engine:** 1,690cc, V twin
- **Weight:** 858lbs (389kg)
- **Power:** 78bhp at 3,500rpm

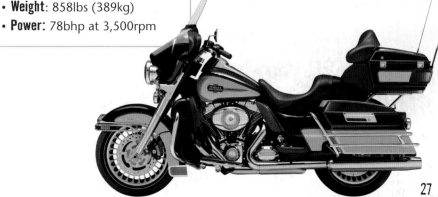

Emergency motorcycles

Some street and touring motorcycles have been adapted for use by police, paramedics and firefighters. They're fast and can dodge city traffic more easily than cars, ambulances and trucks.

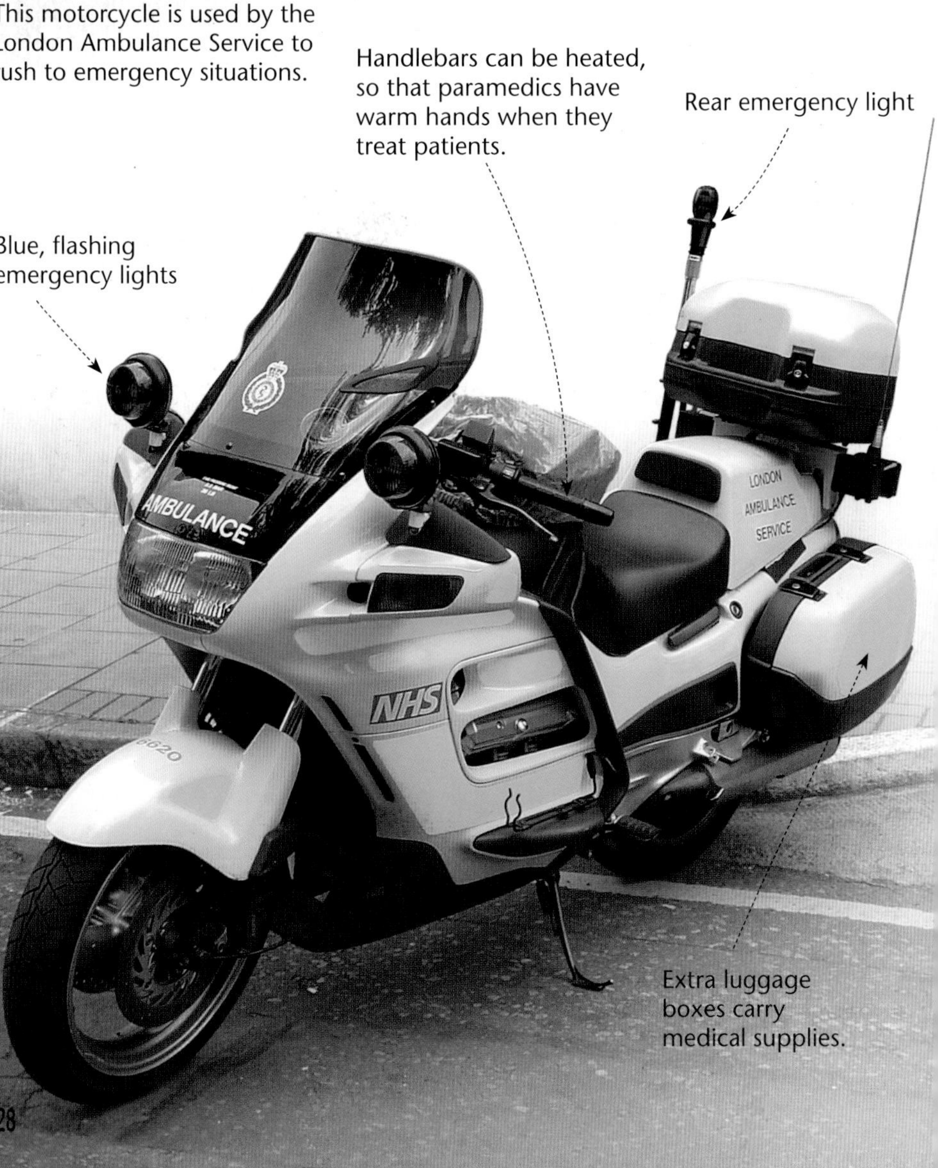

This motorcycle is used by the London Ambulance Service to rush to emergency situations.
Handlebars can be heated, so that paramedics have warm hands when they treat patients.
Rear emergency light
Blue, flashing emergency lights
AMBULANCE
LONDON AMBULANCE SERVICE
NHS
Extra luggage boxes carry medical supplies.

A city-center emergency

A fire breaks out in a narrow city-center alley. Someone contacts emergency services.

Rear emergency light

Hose reel

Water and foam canisters

The fire department decides to send a fire motorcycle.

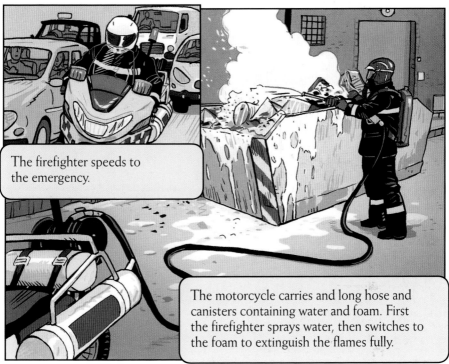

The firefighter speeds to the emergency.

The motorcycle carries and long hose and canisters containing water and foam. First the firefighter sprays water, then switches to the foam to extinguish the flames fully.

29

Cruisers

Cruisers have the style and feel of old classic motorcycles (see pages 72-73), but with powerful, modern engines.

Blackline (Harley–Davidson, USA, 2011)

- **Engine:** 1,584cc, V twin
- **Weight:** 648lbs (294kg)
- **Power:** 75bhp at 3,250rpm

Cruiser riders sit upright with their arms up, and usually their feet in front of them.

Large headlight

Low saddle

A sleek-looking dual exhaust pipe

Footrest

Exposed engine

Commando 961SE (Norton, UK, 2010)

- **Engine:** 961cc, inline 2 cylinder
- **Weight:** 414lbs (188kg)
- **Power:** 80bhp at 6,500rpm

The Commando is sometimes described as a café racer. It's based on a style of 1960s racing bike.

Chief Classic (Indian, USA, 2010)

- **Engine:** 1,721cc, V2
- **Weight:** 728lbs (330kg)
- **Power:** 74bhp at 4,500rpm

Indian Motorcycles have been making Chiefs since 1920. They're among the best-loved American motorcycles.

VT750C Shadow (Honda, Japan, 2010)

- **Engine:** 745cc, V2
- **Weight:** 555lbs (252kg)
- **Power:** 45bhp at 5,500rpm

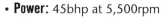

Choppers

Choppers are powerful, large, stretched-out motorcycles. They are sometimes called stripped-down, or naked, motorcycles because they often have no paneling, mirrors, windshields or fenders.

Personalized mirrors

Wide handlebars

This chopper was specially designed and built for a customer.

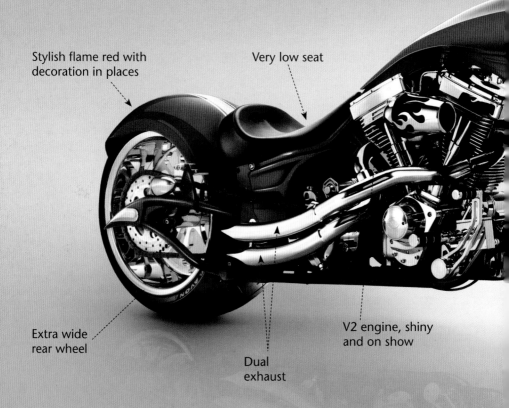

Stylish flame red with decoration in places

Very low seat

Extra wide rear wheel

Dual exhaust

V2 engine, shiny and on show

Chopper riders lean back with their arms and legs stretched out.

The name 'chopper' was first used in the 1950s, when bikers used to chop off unwanted parts of their motorcycles to make them lighter and faster.

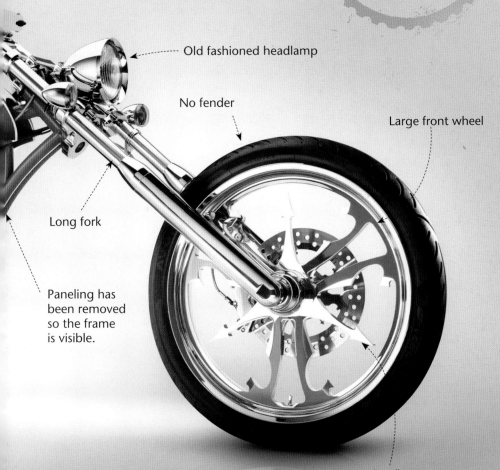

Old fashioned headlamp

No fender

Large front wheel

Long fork

Paneling has been removed so the frame is visible.

Many chopper riders build their own customized motorcycles from scratch.

Personalized chrome spokes on front wheel

Sport bikes

Sport bikes are designed to be among the sleekest, fastest and most powerful vehicles on the road.

Huge fans create winds of up to 310mph (499km/h).

This sport bike is being tested in a wind tunnel. This simulates high-speed riding conditions to test how aerodynamic it is – how smoothly it moves through the air.

These orange leads are electrical sensors that help engineers examine how wind moves around the motorcycle.

The tires run on treadmills that keep the motorcycle in position. Speed readings are sent to a computer for analysis.

Sport riders sit with their hands and head leaning forward and their legs tucked behind them.

Ninja ZX–RR (Kawasaki, Japan, 2009)

- **Engine:** 798cc, inline 4 cylinder
- **Weight:** 326lbs (148kg)
- **Power:** 200bhp at 22,916rpm

Daytona 675 (Triumph, UK, 2010)

- **Engine:** 675cc, inline 3 cylinder
- **Weight:** 408lbs (185kg)
- **Power:** 124bhp at 12,600rpm

Isle of Man TT

One of the biggest sport bike events is the Isle of Man Tourist Trophy (TT) which is held every year. It is a time trial race: the competitors ride in groups, each trying to complete the course in the fastest time.

The TT is a road race – public roads are closed to cars and pedestrians during the race.

The course record, set in 2009 by John McGuinness, riding a Honda motorcycle, is 17 minutes, 12 seconds.

The competition lasts about two weeks, with practice runs, heats and finals for each size of engine.

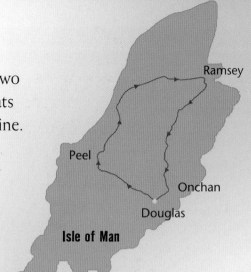

Ramsey

Peel

Onchan

Douglas

Isle of Man

Fans line much of the route to watch the racing. This can be dangerous if a rider crashes into the race barriers.

The Isle of Man is located in the Irish Sea, between Ireland and Great Britain. Each race starts and finishes in the town of Douglas. The course is 38 miles (60km) long and covers towns and countryside, mountain roads and many sharp bends.

Rider Joey Dunlop won the TT a record 26 times. He died during a race in Estonia in 2000.

Super motorcycles

The most powerful, high-tech motorcycles, with capacities of around 1,000cc or more, are super motorcycles. They are very expensive because engineers spend years designing them.

Super motorcycle riders sit in the same position as sport bike riders.

This rider is racing during the 2008 Superbike Supersport World Championships in Doha, Qatar.

Some superbikes are built to ride on public roads; others are only raced in competitions. Bikes only designed for the track are raced in MotoGP events, while modified versions of road superbikes are raced in the Superbike World Championships.

Molded paneling, or fairing, makes super motorcycles especially aerodynamic.

On the next four pages you can see some of the most impressive superbikes around today. They can typically reach speeds of up to 200mph (320km/h).

Super motorcycle information is often top secret, so the statistics on these spreads are approximate.

999 R (Ducati, Italy, 2007)

- **Engine:** 999cc, inline 2 cylinder
- **Weight:** 399lbs (181kg)
- **Power:** 148bhp at 9,750rpm
- **Type:** racing super motorcycle

Road super motorcycles rarely reach their highest speeds because those speeds are illegal on most public highways.

Hayabusa GSX1300R (Suzuki, Japan, 2010)

- **Engine:** 1,340cc, inline 4 cylinder
- **Weight:** 485lbs (220kg)
- **Power:** 172bhp at 9,500rpm
- **Type:** road super motorcycle

1190 RC8 (KTM, Austria, 2010)

- **Engine:** 1,148cc, V2
- **Weight:** 406lbs (184kg)
- **Power:** 152bhp at 10,000rpm
- **Type:** racing super motorcycle

This style of motorcycle is raced at a Superbike World Championship event known as Superstock 1000.

CBR1000RR Fireblade (Honda, Japan, 2011)

- **Engine:** 999cc, inline 4 cylinder
- **Weight:** 439lbs (199kg)
- **Power:** 176bhp at 12,500rpm
- **Type:** road super motorcycle

RSV4 (Aprilia, Italy, 2010)

- **Engine:** 1,000cc, V4
- **Weight:** 406lbs (184kg)
- **Power:** 241bhp at 12,500rpm
- **Type:** racing super motorcycle

Italian racer Max Biaggi won the Superbike FIM World Championship in 2010, riding an Aprilia RSV4.

Organized racing involves different events for sport bikes and super motorcycles depending on their engine capacity. The championships involve many rounds of races at different racetracks around the world.

S 1000 RR (BMW, Germany, 2010)

- **Engine:** 999cc, inline 4 cylinder
- **Weight:** 403lbs (183kg)
- **Power:** 193bhp at 13,000rpm
- **Type:** racing super motorcycle

To help make them extra light, some racing super motorcycles, such as this Moto Guzzi, don't have headlights or mirrors.

MGS-01 Corsa (Moto Guzzi, Italy, 2010)

- **Engine:** 1,225cc, V2
- **Weight:** 423lbs (192kg)
- **Power:** 128hp at 8,000rpm
- **Type:** racing super motorcycle

YZR-M1 (Yamaha, Japan, 2010)

- **Engine:** 998cc, inline 4 cylinder
- **Weight:** 326lbs (148kg)
- **Power:** 200bhp at 12,500rpm
- **Type:** racing super motorcycle

Spanish racer Jorge Lorenzo won the 2010 MotoGP World Championship riding a Yamaha YZR-M1.

Dirt bikes

Dirt bikes are rugged machines that are used in off-road races, Speedway, Motocross, and ice and endurance races.

Dirt bikers often stand up when riding.

Frames made of light metals, such as chromium or aluminum, keep the motorcycles fast.

RXV 4.5 (Aprilia, Italy, 2006)

- **Engine:** 449cc, V2
- **Weight:** 269lbs (122kg)
- **Power:** 60bhp at 13,000rpm

Small fuel tanks carry enough to race but not so much that the heavy fuel slows them down.

E2 250 EXC-F (KTM, Austria, 2010)

- **Engine:** 250cc, single cylinder
- **Weight:** 212lbs (96kg)
- **Power:** 38bhp at 13,500rpm

Knobbed tires give grip over gravel, stones or mud.

Off-road races called trials, on muddy or rocky courses, test a biker's ability and a bike's performance.

This biker, Martin Barr, is taking part in an off-road trial as part of the 2009 European MX2 Motocross Championships.

Notice the googles that protect the rider's eyes from the soil and dust. Find out more about Motocross on pages 48-49.

This Speedway event took place at the Millennium Stadium, Cardiff, in the UK, in 2003.

Speedway

Speedway is a fast and popular type of track racing, using modified dirt bikes. Two teams, with two riders each, race around the course four times. The riders earn points depending on their finishing place.

Speedway motorcycles run on a chemical called methanol, not gasoline. Methanol lets them accelerate really quickly, but is more expensive than gasoline.

When the race is over, the riders let go of the throttle and put their feet on the ground to stop.

Each team competes in 15 races at a day-long event. At the end, the team with the most points wins.

The race is around an oval-shaped, dirt-surfaced track.

Start and finish line

Padded crash barriers, called air fences, surround the track.

Audience seating

47

Motocross

Motocross is a popular type of off-course racing. It involves riding dirt bikes around courses with dirt, mud or grass surfaces. Along the route, there are hills to climb, ledges to jump from and obstacles to avoid.

Riders climb a steep hill while competing in a British Motocross Championship race in Wiltshire, in the UK, 2010.

One type of Motocross event takes place at indoor stadiums and is called Supercross. 20 riders race for 20 laps around courses that include man-made ramps and jumps.

Motocross was originally called scrambling. Now a scramble usually means a race through a wooded area, slipping and sliding along muddy paths and around trees and hedges.

Ice racing

Ice racing is slippery and dangerous. Ice racing motorcycles are fitted with spiked tires that dig into the surface for balance.

These riders are taking part in the Team Ice Racing World Championship final in the Netherlands.

Ice racing motorcycles use methanol as fuel.

The tire studs give the motorcycles more grip as they take corners. They might slip and slide, but they still keep going at average speeds of about 70mph (115km/h).

Most races are held on oval shaped tracks on the icy surfaces of frozen lakes or on winding, frosty, snow-covered roads. But some are held at indoor tracks.

The championships were first held in 1979. The 2010 winner was Russia. They won every year from 2003 to 2010.

The Dakar Rally

The ultimate off-road journey, that tests a rider's strength, skill and determination over a number of days, is known as an endurance race. The most famous one for motorbikes is the Dakar Rally.

Riders race across the Atacama Desert during the 2010 Dakar Rally in South America. The race also involves riding over steep mountains, along coastal roads and through water.

The Dakar is about 5,600 miles (9,000km) long. It starts in late December and lasts 16 days. Some days the racers cover 500 - 600 miles (800 - 1,000km) over 12 hours of intense riding.

The Dakar Rally gets its name from the city of Dakar in Senegal where most of the rallies used to finish.

START PARIS
France
Spain
Ferry from Spain to Morocco.
Morocco
Mauritania
Senegal
DAKAR
FINISH

But since 2009 the rally organizers have chosen routes through South America, instead – although the race is still called the Dakar Rally.

ARICA
Chile
Argentina
BUENOS AIRES
START and FINISH

Doing the Dakar

It takes months to prepare for the Dakar rally. Riders go to the gym to exercise to get fit before race training.

Jacket with built-in water bottle and straw

Then they need to get 'bike fit' – able to ride all day long. Riders enter day long endurance tests to train, riding through mud, over sand and up mountains.

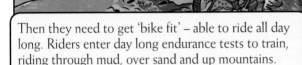

Reinforced suspension

Sand tires

Dirt bikes are modified to cope with the race length and conditions.

BRRRMMM! BRRRMMM!

The race begins early in the morning. When everyone turns on their engines at the start line, the noise is deafening.

Road book

Each day of the rally is broken into stages. The riders navigate the route by following directions from a road book.

TE

Rally cars and huge trucks also enter the race. But, they cause huge dust clouds which reduce visibility.

Some riders have support teams of mechanics. They travel separately and repair the bikes each night. Other riders must fix their bikes themselves before they sleep.

The Dakar camp is known as bivouac and it moves with the race. It's a small town of tents, medical staff, mechanics and organizers. Each day huge planes transport the bivouac to the next night's stop.

Some racers crash, become exhausted or get lost. Rescue helicopters can find them using positioning signals.

Only about a third of the riders make it to the end of the Dakar. They are all awarded medals for the acheivement.

How motorcycles began

When bicycles were invented in the 19th century, engineers began thinking of how to adapt them into powered vehicles.

The larger front wheel was still powered by pedals.

A fire boiler turned water into steam to drive the back wheel.

No brakes

Michaux & Perraux (France, 1868)

A French bicycle company, Michaux and Perraux, designed a bicycle with a rear wheel that was powered by a steam engine.

Roper (USA, 1867)

An American designer, Sylvester Roper, also developed the idea of using a steam engine to power a bicycle.

Inside the saddle was a water tank. A lever was used to pump water to a boiler.

Brake lever

No pedals

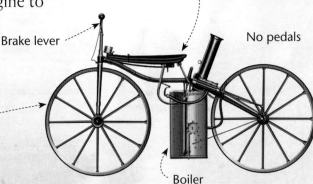

The front wheel turned as the back wheel was powered by the engine.

Boiler

The first motorcycle

In 1885, German inventors Gottlieb Daimler and Wilhelm Maybach created a bicycle powered by a new type of engine. Known as an internal combustion engine, it ran on gasoline not steam. It's considered to be the first true motorcycle.

Handlebars

Leather saddle

Wooden frame

Metal-rimmed wooden wheels

Footrest

Stabilizer wheel

Internal combustion engine

The birth of the modern motorcycle

After 1885, lots of engineers put forward their own ideas.
At first, many just added engines to their old bicycle designs.

Hildebrand & Wolfmüller
(Germany, 1894–1897)

Hildebrand & Wolfmüller
designed and produced
factory-built motorcycles to
sell to the public.

de Dion-Bouton (France, 1897)

A powered tricycle was designed
by the de Dion-Bouton company.
It was fast, but heavy and and less
popular than lighter motorcycles.

Werner (France, 1897)

This motorcycle, designed by
the Werner company, had the
engine positioned over the
front wheel. But this design
made the motorcycles
unstable, so they tended to
crash and frequently
caught fire, too.

Engine

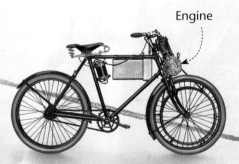

Werner (France, 1900) · Engine

This Werner motorcycle had its engine fitted to the frame between the wheels. It was a well balanced and very popular motorcycle, but it had pedals in case the engine failed.

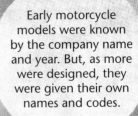

Early motorcycle models were known by the company name and year. But, as more were designed, they were given their own names and codes.

Indian (USA, 1905)

This Indian was one of the first models where the rider started the engine by twisting the grips on the handlebars.

Triumph (UK, 1907)

This Triumph had a thicker metal frame and a bigger engine, but no pedals.

Harley-Davidson, Model 11J (USA, 1915)

This Harley-Davidson bike had heavy tires and a V twin engine. The modern motorcycle was beginning to develop.

Side-by-side

Motorcycles can be fitted with sidecars to carry extra passengers. A sidecar is a specially designed car with one wheel and no engine.

These riders are racing their motorcycles and sidecars in an international Motocross event in Germany.

This passenger is hanging from the sidecar to help keep the motorcycle balanced during a turn.

Today, sidecars are mostly used by collectors and racers. But they used to be quite common for everyday transportation in the days before many people owned cars.

Early sidecars

1915 Triumph Model H

Early sidecars were made of different materials, sold separately and attached to any motorcycle.

Wicker sidecar

1954 Triumph T110 Swallow

Later sidecars were designed to match specific motorcycles and sold as a unit.

Motorcycles at war

During the First and Second World Wars, motorcycles were used as military vehicles. Unlike tanks and trucks, they could race over muddy battlefields and forests and scramble through war zones.

First World War 1914–1918

Douglas 2 (Douglas, UK, 1912–1922)

- **Engine:** 348cc, flat 2 cylinder
- **Top speed:** 40mph (64km/h)
- **Use:** Riders often carried battle updates, and orders, between soldiers and their generals.

Douglas produced around 70,000 military motorcycles during the First World War, more than any other manufacturer.

Two-tier side trolley to carry wounded soldiers

Indian Powerplus (Indian, USA, 1917)

- **Engine:** 984cc, V2
- **Top speed:** 62mph (100km/h)
- **Use:** Special ambulance side trolleys were used to carry wounded soldiers to medical tents.

Bikes in battle

Soldiers called despatch riders carried important paperwork and information from the front line.

Some sidecars carried homing pigeons. When the pigeons were released, they delivered messages to army headquarters.

Map of a typical First World War battlefield

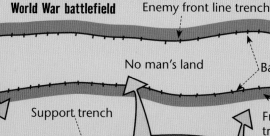

Enemy front line trench

No man's land

Barbed wire

Support trench

Front line trench

Other sidecars carried mounted machine guns. The driver moved around, so that the gunman could aim at different enemy positions.

Ambulance bikes scrambled over battlefields. They were painted with a Red Cross sign so that the enemy knew they weren't a threat.

Royal Air Force
(RAF) despatch
riders leave an
airfield in the UK
to take part in
an off-road training
exercise, 1941.

Second World War 1939–1945

KS750 (Zundapp, Germany, 1940–1948)

- **Engine:** 751cc, flat 2 cylinder
- **Top speed:** 60mph (96km/h)
- **Use:** In battle throughout Europe and in North Africa, on various different terrains.

Machine gun to be used by side-car passenger

2 man crew

Kettenrad (NSU & Stoewer, Germany, 1940–1948)

3 man crew

- **Engine:** 1,488 cc, inline 4 cylinder
- **Top speed:** 46mph (75km/h)
- **Use:** On snowy or sandy terrain to tow large guns and supplies.

Since the Second World War, small military trucks called jeeps have mostly replaced motorcycles in war.

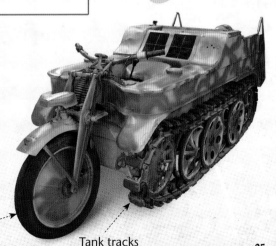

Motorcycle wheel

Tank tracks

Breaking records

The large, flat areas of the Bonneville Salt Flats, USA, are used by experts to ride specialized motorcycles. The ultra smooth surface helps them reach very high speeds of around 360mph (580km/h) in events known as land speed races.

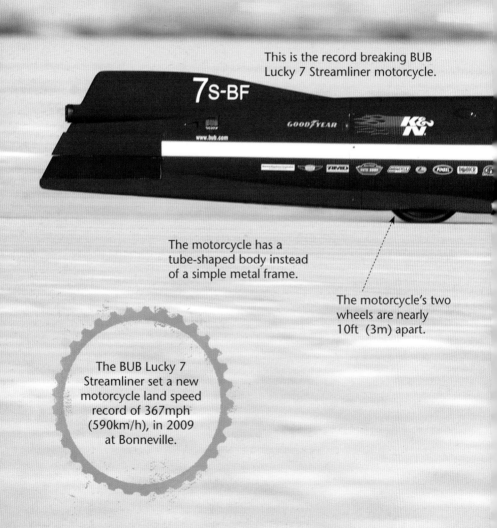

This is the record breaking BUB Lucky 7 Streamliner motorcycle.

The motorcycle has a tube-shaped body instead of a simple metal frame.

The motorcycle's two wheels are nearly 10ft (3m) apart.

The BUB Lucky 7 Streamliner set a new motorcycle land speed record of 367mph (590km/h), in 2009 at Bonneville.

This motorcycle doesn't look anything like a usual motorcycle. But it is defined as a motorcycle in land speed record attempts because it has only two wheels.

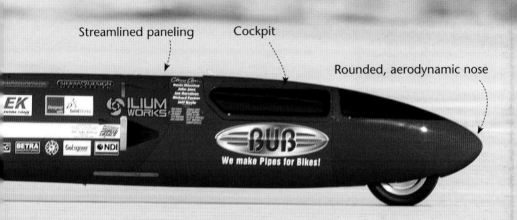

Streamlined paneling

Cockpit

Rounded, aerodynamic nose

Streamliner layout

The powerful V4, methanol-fueled engine sits between the wheels in the middle of the body.

The rider sits in the cockpit at the steering wheel.

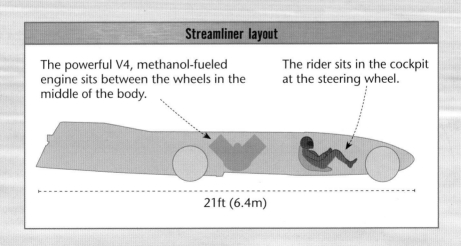

21ft (6.4m)

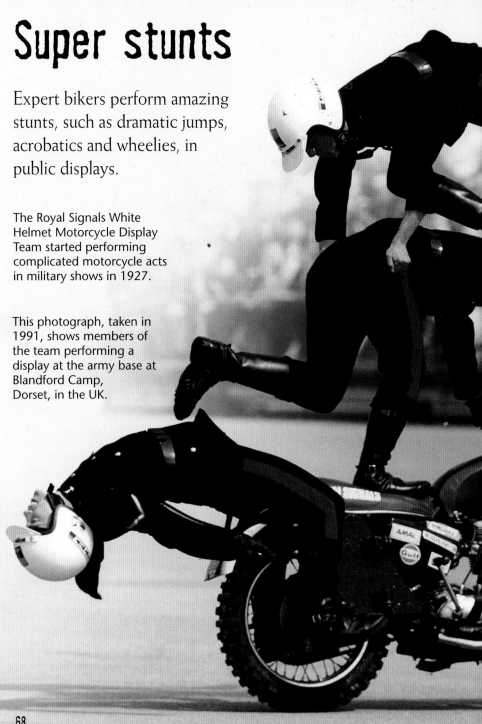

Super stunts

Expert bikers perform amazing
stunts, such as dramatic jumps,
acrobatics and wheelies, in
public displays.

The Royal Signals White
Helmet Motorcycle Display
Team started performing
complicated motorcycle acts
in military shows in 1927.

This photograph, taken in
1991, shows members of
the team performing a
display at the army base at
Blandford Camp,
Dorset, in the UK.

Wall of Death

The Wall of Death is a famous stunt show. The audience stands at the top of a huge barrel-type stage.

Bikers ride at very high speeds around the bottom of the barrel. This creates a force that pushes them against the barrel wall, and lets them ride higher and higher without falling down.

The team is best-known for their balancing acts and fire jumps. They're consulted by film crews who are planning motorcycle stunts for movies, too.

This image was made using time-lapse photography. It combines shots of 17 different moments during a single jump.

Stunt story

Individual stunt riders often stage huge public events to show off their skills. They spend months rehearsing and assessing any dangers to try to make the stunt as safe as possible.

One of the most famous stunt riders was Evel Knievel (1938-2007). He broke 35 bones during his career, including his skull and lower back bone.

Stunt biker Travis Pastrana performed this complicated somersault routine at the 2004 X Games in Los Angeles, USA. The X Games is a series of international extreme sports competitions.

Classic motorcycles

Some bikers restore and ride stylish bikes from the 1930s, 1940s and 1950s, now known as vintage motorcycles. They're often sleek and luxurious with strong, colorful designs and shiny engines.

Scout (Indian, USA, 1949)

- **Engine:** 440cc, vertical twin
- **Weight:** 440lbs (200kg)
- **Power:** Unknown

Streamline KJ (Henderson, USA, 1930)

- **Engine:** 1,300cc, inline 4 cylinder
- **Weight:** 500lbs (227kg)
- **Power:** 40bhp at 4,000rpm

VLD (Harley–Davidson, USA, 1934)

- **Engine:** 1,200cc, V twin
- **Weight:** 408lbs (185kg)
- **Power:** 40bhp at 4,000rpm

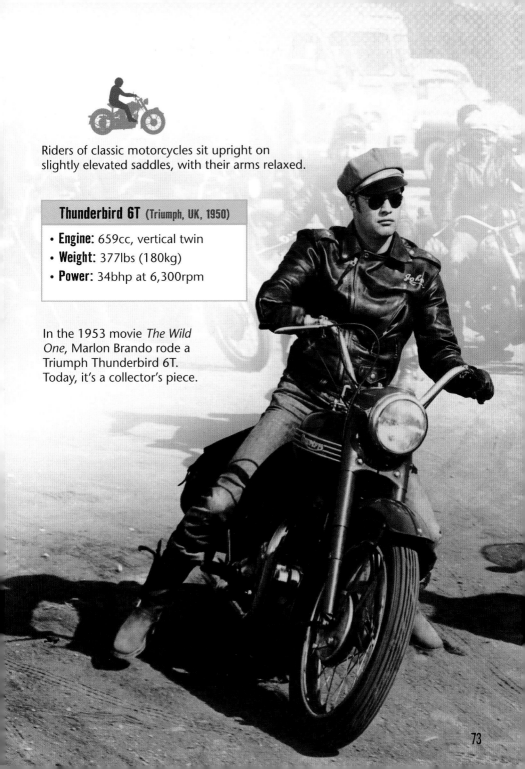

Riders of classic motorcycles sit upright on slightly elevated saddles, with their arms relaxed.

Thunderbird 6T (Triumph, UK, 1950)

- **Engine:** 659cc, vertical twin
- **Weight:** 377lbs (180kg)
- **Power:** 34bhp at 6,300rpm

In the 1953 movie *The Wild One*, Marlon Brando rode a Triumph Thunderbird 6T. Today, it's a collector's piece.

Motorcycles on the internet

There are lots of exciting websites where you can find out more about motorcycles and see them in action. At the Usborne Quicklinks Website you'll find links to some great sites where you can:

- Explore a timeline of motorcycles.
- Watch video clips of the Dakar Rally.
- Learn more about how engines work.
- View clips of races and stunts.

For links to these sites and more go to the Usborne Quicklinks Website at **www.usborne-quicklinks.com** and enter the keyword **motorcycles**.

Here, riders race in the 2009 Road MotoGP Racing World Championship Grand Prix in Monterey, California. Motorcycles raced in the Grand Prix are specially built for the competition and reach speeds of around 200mph (320km/h).

When using the internet please follow the internet safety guidelines displayed on the Usborne Quicklinks Website. The recommended websites in Usborne Quicklinks are regularly reviewed and updated, but Usborne Publishing Ltd. is not responsible for the content or availability of any website other than its own. We recommend that children are supervised while using the internet.

Glossary

The glossary explains some of the words used in this book.
Words in italics have their own entry.

acrobatic A type of *stunt* that involves the biker moving away from or around the bike in mid air before joining it again.

aerodynamic Designed with smooth sides to glide through air. Also known as *streamlined*.

bhp 'brake horse power', a unit to measure the power of an engine.

capacity The total amount of fuel and air drawn into the *cylinders* during one engine cycle, measured in cc or cubic centimeters.

carbon fiber A light, extremely strong material made out of incredibly thin fibers.

chassis The main body of a bike including the *frame*, wheels, *suspension* and brakes.

clutch The part that controls the connection between the engine and the *gearbox*.

counter steering Type of steering needed at high speeds. It involves turning the handlebars in the opposite direction of the turn.

crankshaft The part of an engine that turns the motion of the *pistons* into the rotation of the wheels.

cylinder The metal casing inside an engine that encloses a *piston*.

drag races Short races along straight courses ridden on motorcycles called dragsters.

drive system Part of the engine that uses power from the *gearbox* to turn the rear wheel.

endurance race A long race, that can last for days, that tests a rider's skill and determination.

exhaust Pipe that guides waste gases produced by the engine away from the motorcycle.

fiberglass A strong, light material used for protective helmets.

fork Piece of metal that attaches the front wheel to the *frame*.

frame The skeleton of the bike – different sections of the frame are welded together to make it sturdy.

fuel injection system Part of a motorcycle that mixes fuel with air, before they enter the engine.

gearbox Part of the engine that controls the amount of power sent to the wheels from the engine.

internal combustion engine An engine that is powered by burning fuels such as gasoline, diesel or methanol.

Kevlar Strong, tough man-made material resistant to scrapes and tears.

land speed record Races on specialized motorcycles to try to break the record for fastest land vehicle.

lap Once around a track or circuit.

mass-produced When a product is made in large numbers, in a factory.

methanol A liquid fuel that makes motorcycles go faster than petrol does.

off-road Riding or racing motorcycles on grass, mountains or mud.

paneling Plastic or metal trim that protects parts of machinery and can be decorative. Also known as fairing.

personalization Choosing a bike's design features to suit the rider's personal taste and style.

piston A solid piece of metal in an engine that moves up and down to power the motorcycle.

positioning signals Computer and satellite system used to locate vehicles.

production line The sequence of assembly points in a factory where a motorcycle is built.

rallying A competition in which bikers race from point to point and their times are recorded.

road race A motorcycle race that takes place on public roads.

rpm 'revolutions per minute', a measure of how quickly the *crankshaft* spins and how powerful the engine is.

scooter A small, light and relatively inexpensive street motorcycle.

sidecar A specially designed car that can be attached to the side of a motorcycle to carry passengers or luggage.

spokes Struts from the center of a wheel to the rim.

steam engine An engine powered by the steam produced when water is boiled.

streamlined Designed with smooth sides to glide through air. Also known as *aerodynamic*.

stunt A trick, such as a jump, performed by a skilled motorcycle rider.

suspension Part of a motorcycle that deals with shocks and jolts to give a smooth ride.

track race A motorcycle race that takes place on a purpose-built, enclosed course.

tread pattern The pattern of grooves and marks in the tire that aids grip.

visibility The ease with which a rider can see around him or her, which can be limited by bad weather, fog and sand storms.

wind tunnel A long room used for testing motorcycles. It has massive fans that simulate high-speed riding conditions.

Index

Page numbers marked with an 'a' are found underneath the flap on that page.

Acknowledgements

Every effort has been made to trace and acknowledge ownership of copyright. If any rights have been omitted, the publishers offer to rectify this in any future editions following notification. The publishers are grateful to the following individuals and organizations for their permission to reproduce material on the following pages: (b=bottom, r=right, l=left)

cover © REUTERS/Heino Kalis; **p1, p2-3, p45, p48-49** © Adam Duckworth; **p4 br** © Oleksiy Maysymenko/ Alamy; **p6** © JOHN G. MABANGLO/epa/Corbis; **p8-9** © Rick Friedman/Corbis; **p8a-9b** image supplied courtesy of Triumph Motorcycles Ltd.; **p10, p52-53** © JACKY NAEGELEN/Reuters/Corbis; **p13** image supplied courtesy of BMW Motorrad UK; **p18-19, p23** © Jacek Bilski/photolibrary.com; **p24** image supplied courtesy of Yamaha UK; **p26** image supplied courtesy of Kawasaki; **p28** © UK Emergency Vehicles, www.ukemergency.co.uk; **p30, p59 br** image supplied courtesy of Harley-Davidson Motorcycles; **p32-33** © Rick Chou/TRANSTOCK/ Transtock/Corbis; **p34-35** © A2 Wind Tunnel www.A2WT.com; **p36-37** © Getty Images; **p38-39** © Stringer/ Reuters/Corbis; **p41 br** © image supplied courtesy of Honda (UK) Motorcycles; **p46-47** © Jeff Morgan 08/Alamy; **p50-51** © actionplus sports images; **p57, p72** © Bettmann/CORBIS; **p60-61** © Guntmar Fritz/Corbis; **p64** © M. McNeill/Hulton Archive/Getty Images; **p66-67** © James Weishaar-D&W Images; **p66a-67a** © Leo Mason/Corbis; **p68-69** © Trinity Mirror/Mirrorpix/Alamy; **p70-71** © Bo Bridges/Corbis; **p74-75** © Konstandinos Goumenidis/Icon SMI/Corbis.

Motorbike illustrations p5 bl, p35 and p40-43 © Adrian Dean/F1ARTWORK

All other motorbike illustrations by John S Fox and www.avroart.com

Thanks for advice and additional research material to:

Tony Jakeman at BMW Motorrad UK, Carmela Piretti at Ducati, Mike Morgan at Harley-Davidson Motorcycles, Vivek Syal at Hero Honda, Honda (UK) Motorcycles, Marc Pomerantz at Indian Motorcycle Company, Khal Harris at Jardine International, Catherine Gonzalez at Kawasaki Motorcycles UK Ltd., Ross Walker at KTM UK, Kay Johnson at Norton Motorcycles Ltd., Daniela Riberti at Piaggio, Luke Plummer at Suzuki Motorcycles, Triumph Motorcycles Ltd. and Simon Belton at Yamaha UK. Special thanks also to Joshua Ansell and David Murphy.

Series editor: Jane Chisholm **Series designer:** Zoe Wray
Picture research: Ruth King **American editor:** Carrie Armstrong **Digital design:** John Russell